Merry Christmas!!

Rick Boyer

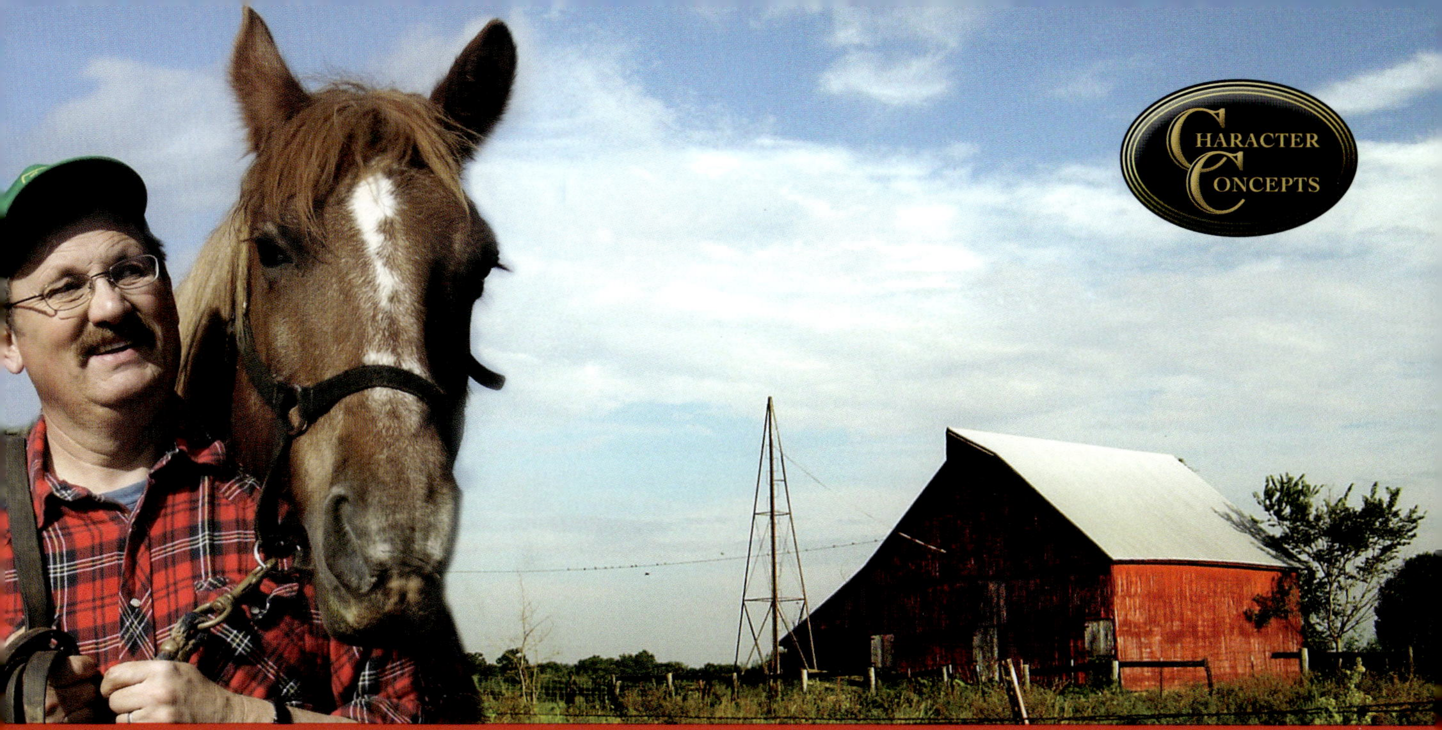

Uncle Rick's Holiday Book

Appreciating the Real Meaning of America's Special Days

by Rick & Marilyn Boyer

First Printing September, 2013

ISBN 978-0-9860433-0-7

published by The Learning Parent
creators of Character Concepts
www.CharacterConcepts.com

Proudly printed in the United States of America by Jostens

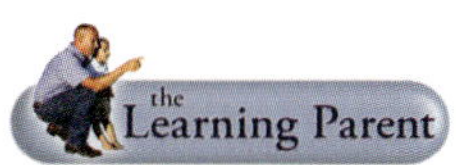

Hey, Little Buddies!

It's Uncle Rick, coming to you from the Little House in the Pasture— where you can hear the birds sing, the cows moo, the horses neigh, and Uncle Rick talk to his little buddies!

I've written this little book just for you. Our holidays are special days and most of them were established to remind us of important events relating to our faith and our national history. Most people today don't understand the real importance of Thanksgiving, Memorial Day, and other special days that used to be celebrated all across America with great joy and reverence. So, I hope the stories I've written for you in this book will tell you some things you didn't know, and that after reading it you will enjoy the holidays, more all throughout the year. Holidays are a very big part of our heritage as Christians and as Americans. Let's give them the honor they deserve, as we recognize the goodness of God and the sacrifices made by those who have gone before us to make America the wonderful place she is.

Love,

Uncle Rick

Uncle Rick's Holiday Book

Unless credited on individual images, photographs and images are either public domain or courtesy of morgueFile.com and stock.xchng. Family photos are courtesy of the Boyer Family.. A complete list of photo credits may be found at: http://characterconcepts.com/store/cms.php?id_cms=29

February 22

George Washington's Birthday

This is the time of year when we celebrate the birthday of one of the greatest men in America's history. His name is George Washington and he has been called "The Father of His Country."

That's a good name for him. George Washington was used by God to win freedom from England for the thirteen English colonies that became the first thirteen American states. Then he went on to lead the effort to unite them into one great nation and even served as the first President of the new nation.

There is a monument to Washington that is over 555 feet high. It is the tallest monument in the Capitol city of America, which is also named after him—Washington, D.C. There is also Washington state, on the Pacific coast and counties, cities, colleges, and many other things named after him. Without a doubt, George Washington was one of the greatest Americans and one of the greatest Christian soldiers who ever lived.

George was born long ago, in 1732. His birthday was February 11th, but when England adopted the new calendar it changed to February 22nd. That is the day we celebrate it now. When I was a little boy, we made a big deal out of George Washington's birthday. Everybody knew about George Washington. There was a picture of him in all my classrooms when I was a little fellow in school. Today there are actually Americans who don't even know who George Washington was. Can you believe it? That shows how little some of us know about our own history. We need to read and study so that we will appreciate the great things God has done in giving us the great heritage of freedom and justice we have in America.

George was the son of Augustine and Mary Washington. Augustine was a well-to-do planter who owned land in the Virginia colony. George had two older half-brothers, Lawrence and Austin. His older half-sister was named Jane. George's father died when George was only eleven years old, but his brother Lawrence partly took his place in George's life. He was George's beloved friend and teacher. Many years later, he would leave George a beautiful plantation called Mount Vernon on the Potomac River in Virginia.

George Washington grew up living the life of the son of a plantation owner, but he was not a spoiled, soft boy. Oh, no! He worked hard and spent a lot of time horseback riding, shooting, and exploring in the woods. He was known as an honest, good-natured young man who was well-liked in the community, honest and dependable, and devoted to his dear mother, Mary. He was tall, strong, and athletic.

George was taught to read by his father and brother Lawrence. He also had other tutors and attended a local school for a short time. He never went to college. Yet he learned well, read a lot of books, and was interested in many things. When he was only seventeen, he was hired by Culpepper County, Virginia, to be its head surveyor.

George was a major in the Virginia militia when trouble started between Britain and France in 1753. Both France and England had colonies in America at that time, and they argued with each other over which country had a right to certain areas. There was an area called the "Ohio country" which both nations claimed. Governor Dinwiddie sent George and his soldiers to warn the French to leave.

But the French soldiers refused to leave Ohio. There were some battles between the British and the French. Some of the Indians joined with the French. Others joined with the British and fought against them. The fighting got worse and soon the French and Indian War was under way.

In 1755, Washington was the highest-ranking American officer to go with the British general, Edward Braddock, on an expedition to drive the French out of the Ohio country. Washington knew that the French and their Indian allies would fight Indian style, hiding behind rocks and trees, shooting from cover. He tried to explain this to General Braddock, but that proud Englishman wouldn't listen to him. He thought that he knew much more about warfare than a young soldier from the woods of Virginia. Washington was afraid that Braddock would lead his troops right into an Indian ambush, and that is exactly what he did.

Braddock was leading his column through a dense wood when suddenly the forest rang out with war whoops and musket fire. Redcoated soldiers fell in their tracks while Washington's buckskin Continentals took cover and fought back Indian style. Braddock's men were sitting ducks for the clever French and Indian sharpshooters. Soon it was clear that the battle was becoming a slaughter.

The Indians were smart fighters. They knew that the men in Braddock's army who rode on horses rather than marching were the officers. They aimed at the officers first, knowing that without leaders, any army is easy to overcome. Before long, George Washington was the only man left in the saddle. Two horses were shot out from under him, yet God protected him from the storm of bullets and he somehow survived.

Braddock had died with a wound in his chest and with all the other officers down, it fell to George to lead their escape from the

Colonel George Washington in 1772

trap. Fighting bravely, George got his men organized and began to retreat. He quickly had Braddock buried in a shallow grave and led his army over the grave so the Indians couldn't find the grave, dig up the body and mutilate it.

President George Washington

Many years later, Washington and a friend were travelling through the area again. They were approached by an old Indian chief who spoke to them through an interpreter. He had been one of the chiefs among the Indians who fought with the French against Braddock on that July day back in 1755. He told Washington that he had instructed his men to fire on Washington when he was the last man on horseback. But though his sharp-eyed braves had tried many times, no bullet had gotten through the supernatural protection of God to kill him. One Indian said that he had shot at Washington seventeen times but could not hit him. It seemed that Washington was protected by a force that bullets couldn't get past!

And indeed he was. God had plans for Washington in the establishment of a Christian nation in the New World. He would not allow him to be killed. In fact, George had written to his brother the day after the battle that, though he had two horses shot from under him, though he had bullet fragments in his hair and four bullet holes in his coat, he had been delivered by Providence to fight another day.

And there were many other days, for twenty years after the Braddock disaster, Virginia and the other colonies were fighting not with the French but with their own countrymen, the English.

The King of England had been treating his subjects in America unfairly. He was not giving them the same rights as other Englishmen. There began to be fights between English soldiers and American settlers. King George could have repaired his relationship with his American subjects, but he seemed too proud. Even though it was against the English Constitution, he grew harsher in the way he treated the Americans. He made them pay taxes that were unfair. He stirred up some of the Indian tribes to attack American settlements. He sent soldiers to enforce his rules, then made the colonists let the soldiers live in their homes and eat their food. If any of the soldiers did something wrong to an American, he couldn't be tried in an American court but had to be sent home to England to face a judge. Justice was rarely done in these cases.

King George did many other illegal and foolish things, but still most Americans wanted to remain English citizens. They didn't want to start a new country, but just to be treated like other Englishmen.

But in April of 1775, British soldiers tried to steal guns and supplies that the Massachusetts militia had stored at the towns of Lexington and Concord. Paul Revere and other riders mounted their horses and spread the word that the British were on the way. They were met by the Minute Men who left their farms, shouldered their guns, and turned out for battle. Even after these battles on April 19, 1775, most of the colonists still wanted to remain loyal to England. But King George would not listen to their pleas. He said he would treat them as conquered foreigners, not English citizens. Soon the War of Independence was on.

George Washington was selected to lead the American army. It seemed an impossible job. The Continental Congress had no money to pay the soldiers or buy them the cannons and ammunition they needed. America had no navy with which to meet the British navy, the most powerful one in the world. Washington won some battles, but he lost most of them in the early days of the war. It was an unequal match between mighty England and the infant nation trying to survive and grow into the United States.

In December of 1777, Washington had led his ragged troops to Pennsylvania to spend the winter. They had been driven out of Philadelphia by the triumphant British and now they retreated to nearby Valley Forge to keep an eye on the British while trying to rebuild their tattered, starving army. There were few tents, no houses, not enough clothing or shoes for the desperate soldiers. Many of them walked with rags around their feet and left bloody footprints in the snow. Wounded men died without adequate medical care. Many more, weakened by starvation and exposure, died from sickness. Hundreds left the camp because they had only promised to stay until the end of 1777, and they were concerned about their hungry families back home.

General Washington at Valley Forge

But by depending on God's guidance through prayer, the great George Washington held his army together. His drill master built up their confidence by training them day after day, showing them that they were becoming better soldiers all the time, despite their sufferings. Then, on Christmas night, 1777, Washington led his men in a surprise attack on Trenton, New Jersey, across the half-frozen Delaware River.

Neither the British nor their hired Hessian soldiers dreamed that an army could move in such horrible winter weather. They never thought that thousands of

General Washington at Trenton

starving, exhausted men could cross an ice-choked river at night, then march nine miles on bleeding feet through an ice storm and even arrive ready to fight. Yet that is what the men of Washington did. The Hessian soldiers were mostly sleeping after celebrating Christmas with feasting and drinking when the ragged Continentals burst upon them. They hardly even put up a fight. And suddenly the Americans had food, guns, and supplies that they had only dreamed of in Valley Forge.

Battle after battle followed and the war dragged on through more difficult, agonizing years. But at last, in 1783, Lord Cornwallis surrendered to Washington at Yorktown in Virginia and the war was over. The colonies were free states and would soon become a nation.

George Washington had proven himself the man to lead that nation. He was urged to organize America into a new country and reign over it as king. George wanted no such thing. He wanted America to be a land where no man was king, but every man could vote for the leaders he wanted. For himself, he wanted to go back to his beloved family and Mount Vernon and be a simple farmer.

But his country called again. He was asked to serve as President of a meeting called the Constitutional Convention. It was to be his job to lead his countrymen once again as they laid the foundation for government. Back he went from Mount Vernon to Philadelphia.

Washington's inauguration

The new Constitution created by Washington, Adams, Franklin, and many other great men still stands as a masterpiece of human organization. It has governed America for over two hundred years while other countries around the world have changed their forms of government time after time. It took a lot of time, argument, and compromise to create a document that all thirteen of the new states would agree to, but God guided Washington and the others. It was done, and while they agreed that it was not perfect, it was something that all the states could accept.

One great question remained still. The new Constitution required that America would have a President. Who would the first President be?

There was little doubt. George Washington was elected by a large majority and served two four-year terms in that office before turning over the responsibility to John Adams, who had served with Washington as his Vice President. Washington returned to his beloved home and settled down to farming life.

One of Washington's generals called him, "First in war, first in peace, and first in the hearts of his countrymen." Two centuries later we still call him the father of our country. He was a good, great, and godly man. I hope all my little buddies will try hard to be like him. America needs you today, as she needed him then.

http://daughterofthegoldenwest.blogspot.com/2012_02_01_archive.html

Spring

Easter • The Resurrection of Jesus

Easter is a very, very special holiday because on Easter we remember one of the greatest miracles God ever did. He brought Jesus back from the dead!

Some people say the birth of Jesus is an even greater miracle than Easter. They say that for God to become man and be born like any other baby is the greatest miracle of all. Well, I don't really know how to compare one miracle with another, but I'm sure you'll agree that both the birth of Jesus and His resurrection are great, wonderful things.

Jesus was laid in a manger when He was born.

Traditional site of Jesus' empty tomb in Jerusalem

I'll bet you already know that Jesus died on a cross to pay for our sins. That means that if we repent of our sins and trust in Him we can be born again—have a brand new life that will last forever in heaven with God. Well, I'll bet you've heard about the first Easter too. But it's a wonderful story and worth telling again. So settle down and get comfortable and let's remember that marvelous morning together.

It was Sunday morning, the first day of the week. A group of women were walking along a dusty road toward the place where Jesus was buried. He had died on Friday, hanging on a cross in agony. Poor Jesus, their beloved Teacher, had been nailed to a rough wooden cross like the two criminals who hung on crosses on either side of Him. This was the good man who had healed so many sick people! He had set people free from demons, made lame people to walk again—even brought dead people to life. So many people had loved Him. Yet He had enemies, people in high places of power. Many of the Pharisees and other religious leaders had hated Him because they were jealous of His power and the way so many people believed that He was really the Messiah, the Son of God. They were finally able to convince Pilate, the Roman governor, that Jesus was a criminal who must be executed.

Jesus dies on the cross.

Poor Jesus! He had never done anything wrong or unkind. Ever! Yet when He was arrested and taken to the home of the high priest, He was beaten savagely. Then He was handed over to the Roman soldiers who whipped Him until the blood ran from hundreds of wounds. They twisted some limbs from a thorn bush into a mock crown and jammed it down onto His head. They punched Him in the face and made fun of Him. Who would ever have believed that the Son of God would be treated that way by people He had created?

They tried to make Jesus carry His own cross up the hill called Calvary but He was too weak from pain and loss of blood. So a stranger was forced to carry it for Him.

Even on the cross, in terrible agony, Jesus was concerned for others. One of the dying thieves repented of his sins and Jesus forgave him. He urged His friend John to care for His mother. Dear, kind Jesus! Everything that He did, He did to obey His heavenly Father and to take care of His people.

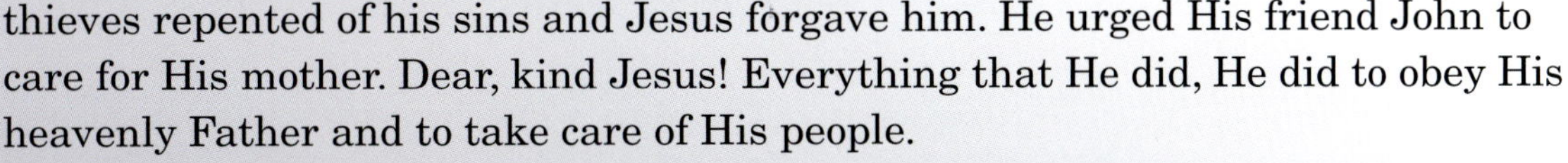

As the sad little group of women walked along, they must have still been amazed that something so terrible had really happened. His mother Mary had given birth to Jesus, loved Him all His life, and then watched in horror as He died. Mary Magdalene had been forgiven of awful sins and delivered from seven demons. She had seen her beloved Master die too. Even though they must have cried so much they thought they could cry no more, I'll bet some of them were dropping their tears in the dust of the road as they walked.

They were carrying expensive spices to embalm his body. A man named Joseph, a rich man from Arimathea had asked Pilate for the body of Jesus. He respected the Lord so much that he had buried Jesus in a garden tomb that he had bought for himself at a great price. Nicodemus, a Jewish leader who once sought Jesus out by night to speak to Him, spent a lot of money for myrrh and aloes to embalm Him. But the two Marys and the other faithful ladies couldn't be content with that. They were going to ask the Roman soldiers to let them do even more for the body of Jesus. They hadn't been able to save His life, but they wanted to do something—anything—to express their love for Him now that He was dead.

Finally, their long, sad walk ended at the garden. They knew where the tomb was, but when they got to it they didn't see any soldiers. They wondered who would roll away the heavy stone that covered the opening of the tomb. But wait! Their eyes were wide with amazement as they saw that the tomb was already open! The stone

Women see the angels at the Jesus' empty tomb.

had been rolled away and there was nothing to keep them away from the body of their beloved Jesus.

Then they were even more astonished when the dim light of the early dawn showed them a man—sitting on the stone itself! But no, it wasn't a man. It was a glorious angel, sent from God! The women were terrified. But the angel's kind voice tells them there is nothing to fear. "Fear not ye," he says, "for I know that ye seek Jesus, which was crucified. He is not here: for He is risen, as He said. Come, see the place where the Lord lay."

Still trembling, but with a strange ray of hope beginning to glow in their hearts, the women tiptoed into the cave. There was no body lying there! A second angel spoke kindly to them: "Why seek ye the living among the dead? He is not here, but is risen: remember how He spake unto you when He was yet in Galilee, saying, The Son of Man must be delivered into the hands of sinful men, and be crucified, and the third day rise again. Go your way," he told them, "tell His disciples and Peter that He goeth before you into Galilee: there shall ye see Him, as He said unto you."

The same women who had entered the tomb on tiptoe burst from it, laughing and crying at the same time. Their eyes were wide and their breath couldn't seem to catch up with them as they stumbled out of the garden in their haste and headed back toward Jerusalem. They must speak to Peter and the other leaders of the disciples. They must tell them what the heavenly messenger had said. Their Master was alive!

It was still early morning when they burst into the house where the disciples were staying. It was a tired and worn-looking group of men, most of whom had slept little, who met the breathless women at the door. They tried to understand what the ladies were telling them, but they were all out of breath and talking all at the same time. Finally, the story came out.

"Jesus is alive! We saw angels! The tomb was open and the soldiers were gone! The angels said He's risen! He's alive! When He used to tell us that He would die and live again, that's just what He meant! It wasn't a parable or a riddle—that's just what He meant to do! The angels said so!"

The sad, tired men couldn't believe what they were hearing. These poor, exhausted women had been through all the suffering they themselves had. They had been shocked at watching Jesus die. They had been through sleepless nights. They, too, were in fear for their lives as the Jewish leaders wanted to get rid of all the disciples along with Jesus, their leader. Surely their eyes had been playing tricks on them.

detail from "The Disciples Peter and John Running to the Sepulcher on the Morning of the Resurrection" by Eugène Burnand, c.1898.

But still, Peter and John wanted to see for themselves. Now they started out at a run for the garden tomb. John was a little faster and arrived at the tomb first, hesitating outside the dark mouth of the cave. Peter ran up, panting, and impulsively shoved past his friend to go inside.

There were the graveclothes in which Jesus had been wrapped. Even the cloth that had covered His head was lying there, neatly rolled up. But there was no body in the grave. It was empty. John entered the tomb a moment later. He looked at the graveclothes and knew in his heart that a miracle had taken place. But neither he nor Peter fully understood. Jesus would soon appear to them and open their eyes to the marvelous truth of His resurrection. But they had not yet seen their risen Lord.

As Peter and John headed back toward Jerusalem talking excitedly, a single figure lingered by the grave, weeping softly. Humble little Mary Magdalene had evidently followed the men and made the weary trip from the city a second time. Her emotions must have been very confused indeed. She was probably still in shock from the horrors she had witnessed just a couple of days before. She had seen an angel—a real angel! And he had given her news so wonderful and so strange that those who heard could not entirely accept it. She was exhausted and confused and hopeful all at the same time. She would pause and rest a moment before starting home. She would cry for a while, tears of pain and weariness and hope and joy all mixing together. She had been told by a heavenly messenger that her beloved Jesus had risen from the

Jesus appears to Mary at the tomb.

dead, but she couldn't quite grasp it all. Not yet. But she soon would.

As the voices of Peter and John faded into the distance, she felt a strange urge to look again into the tomb. There sat two angels, right where the head and feet of Jesus had been. They kindly asked, "Woman, why are you weeping?"

Mary answered, "Because they have taken away my Lord, and I don't know where they have laid Him." She sniffled quietly. Then she heard a third voice, this one from behind her. It repeated the angels' question.

Mary turned, not knowing who had spoken but assuming it was the man who took care of the garden and the graves. "Sir, if you have carried Him away, tell me where you have laid Him, and I will take Him away."

She still didn't understand. Her eyes had not yet been opened to the truth. But when that gentle voice spoke her name, suddenly she knew. It was Jesus!

"Mary!" He said, lovingly.

"Teacher!" she answered, her tearful eyes suddenly wide with delight and relief as she threw herself toward Him and clung to Him in worship.

"Stop clinging to me, Mary," He said in His kind voice. "I have not yet gone up to My Father. But go and tell My brothers that I am going to Him."

The Bible doesn't tell us a lot of details about what happened then, but I'll bet Mary's tears were suddenly dry as Jesus made everything clear to her. Apparently she was the first one to really get it. Jesus was really alive! She had seen Him with her own eyes. I'll bet she was surprised that she could bring herself to leave Him—but she could, because all of a sudden she understood that everything was all right and this was not the end, but the beginning.

http://www.morethings.com/god_and_country/jesus/resurrection_jesus_photo_gallery05.htm

Mary was tired. She was very, very tired. But I'll bet that suddenly that weariness fell away and that her joy gave wings to her feet. I'll bet she skimmed over that dusty road back to the city faster than she would have ever believed she possibly could. Again she arrived at the house where the disciples were staying. Again she breathlessly blurted out amazing news.

"I saw Him! I've seen the Teacher!" Her face was aglow from joy and the exertion of running.

Peter seeing the risen Christ for the first time

The Bible doesn't say whether the disciples believed Mary this time or not. But they found out for themselves that very evening, because as they were shut up together behind locked doors "for fear of the Jews," Jesus appeared right in their midst! He showed them His hands and His side. The gaping, raw wounds from the nails and the spear were still there. Those were the marks of His love for them and His power over death.

What a hubbub there must have been in that room then! What shouts of joy and tears of relief. What a confused babble of voices, tearful, amazed men hugging each other and the Lord. What hope and happiness!

Scripture tells us that Jesus appeared to His disciples again and again for several weeks, then rose into heaven from the Mount of Olives as His disciples looked on. And then began the wonderful events recorded in the Book of Acts as the disciples took the good news of their Lord's death and resurrection to the uttermost part of the earth. And that story is still going on today, and will go on until Jesus comes again.

Now, my dear young friends, comes the most important question in the world: does the resurrected Jesus live in your heart? Have you confessed your sins and received Jesus as your Savior and Lord? It's one thing to know about Jesus and another to be truly born again in Him. If you don't understand this, ask your Mom and Dad. They'd love to talk to you about it.

May 30 Memorial Day

Memorial Day is always celebrated on the last Monday of May. That's so that many working people can enjoy a three-day weekend to be with their families and celebrate the day. There are a lot of picnics, cookouts and fun of all sorts.

But fun is not really what Memorial Day is all about. So today, I want to tell you the true story of Memorial Day. It's a very important day in America's history and we should all remember why we recognize it.

I don't really know where the first Memorial Day observance was held. Several towns in America claim to be where it started. But there are some things we do know about it. We know that it started because of the War Between the States. You may know that war is also called the Civil War. It happened between 1861 and 1865. Several of the states in the southern part of America wanted to leave the Union and start a new country called the Confederate States of America. The national government didn't want them to leave and break America into two pieces. So the government sent armies into the South to force the Southern states to stay.

In the end, the Union won. But there were many thousands of men killed on both sides. It was especially sad in the South, where most of the battles had been fought. The families on both sides had lost their fathers, husbands, brothers and sons. But in the South, many of their cities had been destroyed too, because of the terrible battles that had been fought there. Hundreds of thousands of people lost their homes, jobs and farms. Many were desperate and starving.

But the people of both sides were proud of the men who had fought in the war. The Northerners felt that their men had fought to keep America together and to end slavery in America. The Southerners felt that their men had fought for the rights of the states to make their own decisions, without the federal government telling them what to do. Both sides believed they were fighting for freedom. What a strange war!

http://westvirginiaville.com/wp-content/uploads/2011/03/Brother-vs-Brother-Richwood-WV-1910s-.jpg

Two brothers, Civil War veterans: one fought for the South, one fought for the North. (Photo taken in 1910.)

Just about a year after the war was over, the women of Columbus, Mississippi gathered at the local graveyard. It was called Friendship Cemetery. I don't know where that name came from, but it must have seemed kind of ironic on that day because there were many Civil War soldiers buried there and they were from both armies. **Think of that! Enemies were buried together in Friendship Cemetery.**

The ladies of Columbus were there that day to put flowers on the graves of the Confederate soldiers. At the same time, ladies all across the South were decorating local graves as well. I'll bet most of those ladies had sons or brothers or fathers or husbands buried there. And I'll bet others had loved ones who had died in battles far away from home and had been buried on the battlefield. They would never come home again. That often happened in those days.

http://www.historymarkersofms.com/Lowndes/Columbus/FriendshipCemetery1.jpg

Friendship Cemetery Historical Marker, Columbus, Mississippi

It's not hard to imagine those ladies of Columbus, young and old, as they slowly moved among the gravestones and wooden headboards with the names of soldiers on them, stooping to place flowers here and there where a loved one lay in his grave. Sad, thin faces looked out through faded bonnets, telling the story of grief and poverty. Girls decorated graves of brothers and fathers. Weeping young women placed flowers above the bodies of husbands. Older women thought of their lost sons and dropped a tear with a flower from time to time. Such a sad day! They were proud of their men for having given their lives in defending their state and town from invading Federal armies, but oh, the grief in those hearts.

Someone had an idea, maybe at the cemetery. Or, maybe somebody thought of it as they were planning ahead on meeting together there. At any rate, these grieving women thought of others who were grieving at the same time, and not just in the South. There were mothers and daughters and sisters and wives up north too, who would never receive their men back from war. There were broken hearts in places hundreds of miles away, and some of those families would never even know how their boys died or where they were buried. They could never put flowers on the loved one's grave.

So the ladies of Columbus took it on themselves. They placed flowers on the graves of the Yankee soldiers as they were decorating the graves of their own boys. No soldier's final resting place should be neglected because he had died far from home. Perhaps some Northern woman was even now dropping a flower on the grave of some Mississippi boy who had died on the field at Gettysburg or Antietam away up north.

http://www.historymarkersofms.com/Lowndes/Columbus/Confederate_Decoration_Day.JPG

Confederate Decoration Day Historical Marker

Several cities in America claim credit for the first memorial observations that turned into the national holiday we know as Memorial Day. One of those is Columbus' sister city, Columbus, Georgia. In the spring of 1866 the Ladies Memorial Association of Columbus, Georgia passed a resolution to set aside one day annually to memorialize the Confederate dead. The secretary of the association was directed to author a letter inviting the ladies in every Southern state to join them in the observance. The letter was written in March of 1866 and sent to all of the major cities in the South.

The date chosen for the holiday was April 25, 1866. That was the first anniversary of Confederate General Johnston's final surrender to General Sherman at Bennett Place, North Carolina. For many in the South, that marked the official end of the war.

On April 25, 1866, tens of thousands of Southern women commemorated the first Confederate Memorial Day. But some in the northern portions of the South didn't have flowers because they weren't blooming yet where they lived. So they selected dates later in the spring to hold their first Confederate Memorial Days.

But according to the Library of Congress, it was Columbus, Mississippi that first officially decided to annually decorate the graves of soldiers from both sides. It really doesn't matter, does it? **What matters is that we remember and honor those who died for causes they believed in.**

Soon, the idea of a day for decorating soldiers' graves spread north. There was a veterans' organization in the North called the Grand Army of the Republic. Union General John A. Logan was the commander-in-chief. He ordered that his organization would honor the war dead, too. According to General Logan's wife, he followed the example of the Confederate Memorial Day. She wrote that Logan said "it was not too late for the Union men of the nation to follow the example of the people of the South in perpetuating the memory of their friends who had died for the cause they thought just and right." General Logan chose May 30, 1868, for the first Decoration Day, as he called it.

http://www.urngarden.com/cremationblog/2008/05/25/memorial-day-vintage-postcards/

Decoration Day postcard with images of Generals Ulysses S. Grant and Robert E. Lee

Gradually, Decoration Day began to be called Memorial Day. Then, almost fifty years after the Civil War, America found itself caught up in another terrible conflict, World War I. Again many American boys died far from home. From that time on, Americans began to decorate the graves of all soldiers on Memorial Day rather than just those who died in the Civil War. And many people began to take advantage of their Memorial Day visits to the cemetery to also decorate the graves of loved ones who were not killed in wars.

Memorial Day wasn't officially recognized as a national holiday by law until 1968. Its date was also changed from May 30 to the last Monday in May, which is when we celebrate it now.

So now little buddies, you know the story of Memorial Day. I hope you enjoy it with your families. And I hope that when the day comes around each year, you will remember and honor those who have given their lives to keep America free.

Library of Congress: http://www.loc.gov/pictures/resource/cph.3g06266/

World War I Memorial Day Poster in memory of American soldiers in all wars from 1775 through 1917

Francis Miles Finch, a Northern judge who wrote poetry as a hobby, was inspired by the Southern ladies who took care of the graves of the soldiers buried in Friendship Cemetery regardless of whether they were Union or Confederate. Here is his poem, which was published in September, 1867.

http://www.whatsoproudlywehail.org/curriculum/the-american-calendar/the-blue-and-the-gray

THE BLUE AND THE GRAY

by Francis Miles Finch

*By the flow of the inland river,
Whence the fleets of iron have fled,
Where the blades of grave-grass quiver,
Asleep are the ranks of the dead:
Under the sod and the dew,
Waiting the judgment-day;
Under the one, the Blue,
Under the other, the Gray.*

*Those in the robings of glory,
Those in the gloom of defeat,
All with the battle-blood gory,
In the dusk of eternity meet;
Under the sod and the dew,
Waiting the judgment-day;
Under the laurel the Blue,
Under the willow, the Gray.*

*From the silence of sorrowful hours
The desolate mourners go,
Lovingly laden with flowers
Alike for the friend and the foe;
Under the sod and the dew,
Waiting the judgment-day;
Under the roses, the Blue,
Under the lilies, the Gray.*

*So, with an equal splendor,
The morning sun-rays fall,
With a touch impartially tender,
On the blossoms blooming for all;
Under the sod and the dew,
Waiting the judgment-day;
Broidered with gold, the Blue,
Mellowed with gold, the Gray.*

*So, when the summer calleth,
On forest and field of grain,
With an equal murmur falleth
The cooling drip of the rain:
Under the sod and the dew,
Waiting the judgment-day,
Wet with the rain, the Blue
Wet with the rain, the Gray.*

*Sadly, but not with upbraiding,
The generous deed was done,
In the storm of the years that are fading
No braver battle was won:
Under the sod and the dew,
Waiting the judgment-day;
Under the blossoms, the Blue,
Under the garlands, the Gray*

*No more shall the war cry sever,
Or the winding rivers be red;
They banish our anger forever
When they laurel the graves of our dead!
Under the sod and the dew,
Waiting the judgment-day,
Love and tears for the Blue,
Tears and love for the Gray.*

Friendship Cemetery, Columbus, Mississippi

http://www.texansinthecivilwar.com/Cemeteries/friendship.jpg

June 14
Flag Day

I want to tell you a little story today about a holiday that a lot of people forget. It's called Flag Day and it is celebrated on June 14.

Flag Day was first officially declared by President Woodrow Wilson on May 30, 1916. But its roots go back to the very beginning of America. It was on June 14 in 1777 that the Continental Congress passed a resolution "that the flag of the thirteen United States be thirteen stripes, alternate red and white; that the union be thirteen stars, white in a blue field, representing a new constellation." It was the first American flag!

When the Continental Congress passed the resolution to create the flag, there wasn't an American nation yet. The Constitution hadn't yet been written, and it is the Constitution that defines what our nation is and how it is put together. That Congress was just a meeting of representatives from the thirteen English colonies who had united together to defend themselves against the tyranny of the English King and Parliament and gain their independence as free states. That's why they were called the United States.

When Captain William Driver was presented with one of these thirteen-star flags in 1831, he called it "Old Glory." That nickname has stuck and we still refer to Old Glory today. That's a wonderful name for the symbol of our freedom, isn't it?

Captain William Driver: http://www.tnportraits.org/30121-driver.htm

Captain William Driver, who coined the nickname "Old Glory" for the American flag

President Wilson, in his declaration in 1916, wanted to make Flag Day an official holiday and see it celebrated in every community in America. He thought that it would be good to celebrate the birth of our national flag with patriotic activities. He wanted to see Americans united in patriotism and express their agreement on the principles of freedom and justice that make America great.

Today, 236 years later, there are fifty stars on our flag, representing the fifty states that now make up our country. Flag Day isn't an official federal holiday, and it doesn't get as much attention as some of our other holidays. I guess that's because it's so close to Independence Day on July fourth which is our main patriotic holiday. But I wanted you to know about it, because I love our flag and the freedom and justice that it stands for. I hope you love the flag too, and that Flag Day is a special day at your house.

IN CONGRESS, JULY 4, 1776.

The unanimous Declaration of the thirteen united States of Ameri

July 4
Independence Day

Independence Day is one of my favorite times of the year! That's the day, July 4th, when we celebrate the signing of the Declaration of Independence and the birth of America. You know, you and I are so blessed to be Americans. We have much more freedom in our country than most people in the world ever know. Our Constitution, especially the Bill of Rights, was established for the purpose of protecting the rights of citizens and limiting the power of government. That's the reason you and I can do and say whatever we choose as long as we don't hurt somebody else by doing so.

The men who started the United States (we call them our Founding Fathers) were English citizens living in North America in the 1700's. They lived in thirteen colonies along the coast of the Atlantic Ocean from New Hampshire in the north to Georgia in the south. The first English colony in America was Jamestown in Virginia. It was established in 1607. The second one was Plymouth in Massachusetts, founded in 1620. That's the one the Pilgrims started.

The other eleven English colonies followed in later years, with Georgia established last in 1733. The people who lived in the colonies came as Englishmen and intended to always be Englishmen. But before long, there was trouble between the colonies and their home country.

King George and the Parliament (sort of like our Congress) started doing things and making laws that weren't fair to the citizens in the American colonies. The King sent soldiers to the colonies and forced the colonists to provide them with places to live in their own homes. He allowed American sailors to be kidnapped from their ships and forced to serve on British navy ships against their will. He stopped some of the American courts from punishing criminals and settling arguments between citizens. He imposed taxes on the colonists without letting them have any part in deciding about them. He seized guns and ammuntion that the colonists had stored to protect themselves. He even stirred up some of the Indians to attack the colonies!

You've heard about the fights between the Patriots and the British soldiers at Lexington and Concord in Massachusetts. That was in 1775. The British had heard that the colonists had guns stored at Concord and that Patriot leaders, John Hancock and Samuel Adams, were staying at a friend's home in Lexington. So the British sent soldiers out to capture Adams and Hancock and take the arms and ammunition stored at Concord.

But Paul Revere, William Dawes, and other Patriots rode through the countryside, warning everyone that the British were on their way. When the Redcoats arrived at Lexington at daybreak on April 19th, Adams and Hancock had made their escape and the countryside was swarming with Minutemen on their way to stop the British.

Even after these battles, most Americans were still loyal to England and only asked for their rights as Englishmen. But the King wouldn't listen. And when the colonists sent him the Olive Branch Petition asking for peace between the colonies and the mother country, he replied that he intended to treat the American colonies like a foreign country to be defeated and controlled by England. The next year, representatives from all the thirteen colonies met in Philadelphia and signed the Declaration of Independence. That Declaration told the world that the colonies no longer belonged to England, but were free and independent states.

Signing of the Declaration of Independence, July 4, 1776

Independence Hall, Philadelphia, Pennsylvania, where the Declaration of Independence was signed

The King didn't take that lying down. He sent more English soldiers to fight the Americans and even hired Hessian soldiers from Germany to help. But the Patriots won the War of Independence and a few years later the colonies passed the Constitution, making them one nation—the United States of America.

The independence of America was built on the truth of the Bible, that all people are equal before God and have rights given by Him that no other man should violate. Most people in the colonies worshiped God and believed in the Bible and most leaders in the colonies were God-fearing men. Also, God had sent a great revival called the Great Awakening in the years before the War of Independence that had brought salvation to many thousands of people under the preaching of George Whitefield, Jonathan Edwards, and other preachers.

So it was that from the early days of the colonial period, when the Pilgrims started the Plymouth colony as a Christian community, until over one hundred fifty years later when the Founding Fathers wrote the Declaration of Independence based on our God-given inalienable rights, God was preparing to build a Christian nation based on His principles. And that's why America has worked so well. That's why we have so much freedom and justice in our country.

Minuteman Statue, Lexington, Massachusetts

And that's why so many people from other countries come to live in America every year.

God's ways work. I hope you will obey God in your life so that He can make you a happy and profitable servant of His, all your days. And I hope you will always be patriotic and work hard to keep God's ways known and honored in America so that He can bless our country. May America always be the land of the free and the home of the brave.

Have a great Independence Day, and never forget that freedom is a gift from God.

September 14
The Star-Spangled Banner

http://www.squidoo.com/U-S-Flags?utm_source=google&utm_medium=imgres&utm_campaign=framebuster

The American Flag with 15 stars and 15 stripes which flew over Fort McHenry during the War of 1812.

I'll bet you've sung "The Star-Spangled Banner" many times. It's our National Anthem and it's played at ball games, patriotic celebrations and other special occasions. I love that song! I'll bet you love it too.

But do you know where it came from? Maybe you thought it was written during the Revolutionary War, when America won her independence from England. But no, that's not the case. It was actually written during another war with England, the War of 1812.

The British had invaded America. In Washington, D.C., they had burned the White House and the Capitol building. Then they sailed up to attack Fort McHenry at Baltimore, Maryland.

Francis Scott Key was a Maryland lawyer. When his friend Dr. Beanes and some other men were taken prisoner by the British and held on board one of their ships, he found out which ship they were on and got permission to go aboard to arrange for the release of the Americans. This was on September 13 (that's my birthday, by the way), 1814. He was treated honorably by the British officers and was successful in gaining his friends' freedom. But he was not allowed to leave the ship that night because the British had already begun firing at nearby Fort McHenry and Key had learned too much of British battle plans.

So all through the night, Francis Scott Key watched anxiously through the smoke and fog to see whether the fort was still in American hands. He knew that as long as he could see the flag flying above the fort's walls, the Americans had not surrendered.

Before the sun went down, the flag was easy to see. But once darkness came, it was only by the occasional "rocket's red glare" that he could get a glimpse of Old Glory still waving above the fort.

Francis Scott Key aboard the British warship watching the bombardment of Fort McHenry, September 14, 1814.

http://3.bp.blogspot.com/-o5NE9qicx4Q/UBICOqSJ_RI/AAAAAAAAAC_8/slh-N-6YH_I/s1600/Francis-Scott+Key.jpg

Francis Scott Key

Finally morning dawned. And there, above the fort's ramparts, still floated the stars and stripes to show that the fort had held out. The British gave up the fight.

Later Key remembered those early morning moments of relief, pride in his country and thankfulness to God: "Then, in that hour of deliverance, my heart spoke. Does not such a country, and such defenders of their country, deserve a song?" It was then that he pulled an envelope from his pocket and began to compose the poem that became our National Anthem.

Francis Scott Key, like most of our early patriots, was a dedicated Christian. Here are a couple of things he said about his faith:

Nothing but Christianity will give you the victory. Until a man believes in his heart that Jesus Christ is his Lord and Master... his course through life will be neither safe nor pleasant. My only regret is that I was so long blinded by my pleasures, my vices and pursuits, and the examples of others that I was kept from seeing, admiring, and adoring the marvelous light of the gospel.

The patriot who feels himself in the service of God, who acknowledges Him in all his ways, has the promise of Almighty direction, and will find His Word in his greatest darkness.

Isn't it wonderful to know that our National Anthem was written by a man like Francis Scott Key?

http://www.baltimoresun.com/entertainment/sun-magazine/bal-50-objects-that-define-baltimore-pictures-20130430,0,507424.photogallery

Handwritten text of Francis Scott Key's poem, originally entitled "The Defense of Fort McHenry." Original on display at the Maryland Historical Society

October 12
Columbus Day

Does your family celebrate Columbus Day? All of us should. Christopher Columbus made the long and dangerous voyage across the Atlantic Ocean looking for a shorter way to reach Oriental countries that European countries wanted to do business with. He thought he could find a route across the ocean that would be shorter and faster than the old slow way of traveling thousands of miles by land. But on his first voyage he bumped into a little island off the coast of Florida. And that was the beginning of the settlement of America.

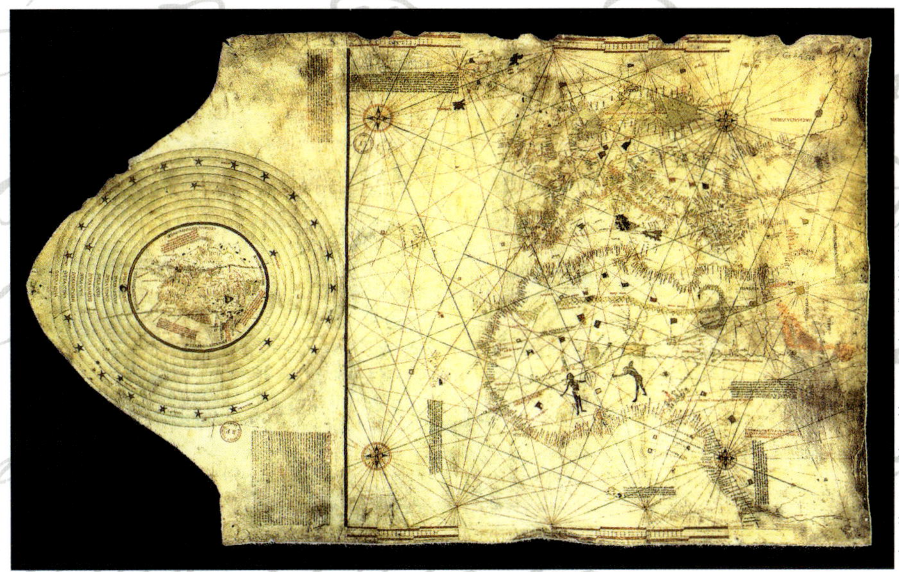
http://ancientworldmaps.blogspot.com/search/label/15th%20century

The "Columbus map" which perhaps was drawn by Christopher Columbus and his brother Bartolomeo in Lisbon around 1490 before the discovery of the New World, showing the known world in their time.

Other explorers had come to North America before, so Columbus wasn't the first European to come here. But he was the first one to really spread the news about the New World across the countries of Europe. After that, several countries began to send people to establish permanent colonies on this continent. England was one of those countries, and the English settlements were the most

Drawing of the *Pinta*, one of the three ships which sailed to the New World with Christopher Columbus.

Map drawn by Venetian monk Fra Mauro in 1450, the first known modern world map

Christopher Columbus

lasting and successful. That's why we speak English in America today.

A lot of people thought that Columbus was crazy when he talked about sailing west to get to countries that had always been reached by land travel going east. They also thought that there were dragons, sea monsters, whirlpools and waterfalls far out in the uncharted oceans that would destroy ships and sailors. It was true that it was a very dangerous thing to try to do.

But Columbus believed that God was leading him to do it. He wrote:

> [O]ur Lord opened to my understanding (I could sense His hand upon me) so it became clear to me that it was feasible. . . . All those who heard about my enterprise rejected it with laughter, scoffing at me. . . . Who doubts that this illumination was from the Holy Spirit? I attest that He, with marvelous rays of light, consoled me through the holy and sacred Scriptures . . . they inflame me with a sense of great urgency. . . . No one should be afraid to take on any enterprise

in the name of our Savior if it is right and if the purpose is purely for His holy service. . . . And I say that the sign which convinces me that our Lord is hastening the end of the world is the preaching of the Gospel recently in so many lands.

Replica of the *Santa Maria,* Columbus' flagship.

http://www.marineinsight.com/marine/life-at-sea/maritime-history/christopher-columbus-ships-vessels-that-discovered-america

Columbus didn't have enough money to buy and equip three ships to sail across the Atlantic. He convinced the King and Queen of Spain to give him the money he needed. They did it hoping to increase their buying and selling with the nations of the Orient. But Columbus believed that he had been led by God to take the Christian faith to countries where Christ was still unknown.

Columbus was successful. His exploration led to the establishment of many European colonies, most of which were Christian in their laws and values. That's why we should celebrate Columbus Day. It honors the memory of a man who was used by God to establish a new Christian nation now called the United States of America.

Columbus and his crew land in the New World, October 12, 1492

November 11
Veterans' Day

November 11 is Veterans' Day. Do you know what it's all about? A lot of people don't.

America was involved in a terrible war early in the twentieth century. For years after the war, it was called the Great War because it was so big, involved so many different countries and caused so much death and destruction. But then in the 1940's, America fought a war that was even bigger. The two wars became known as World War I and World War II. World War I took place between 1914 and 1918. America got involved in 1917 and the war ended in November of 1918. In that nearly two-year period, 110,000 Americans died from battle wounds or disease.

The war ended on November 11, 1918. The warring countries agreed to an "armistice" which is an agreement to stop fighting. The next year, President Woodrow Wilson declared that November 11 of each year would be celebrated as Armistice Day to celebrate the end of the fighting. It was a day to celebrate peace and honor the sacrifices of those who had fought in the war.

But then along came the second World War in the 1940's. And after that, the Korean War in the 1950's. It no longer seemed right to celebrate Armistice Day and not recognize the end of the other two wars as well as the veterans who had served in them. So in 1954, President Dwight Eisenhower signed a law to rename Armistice Day and call it Veterans' Day. The day would now be used to celebrate the service of all veterans in all of America's wars.

And that's why we have Veterans' Day today. But there's more to the story!

The body of the Unknown Soldier being returned from the Europe, November 9, 1921

Have you ever heard of the Tomb of the Unknown Soldier? It is a national monument in Washington, D.C. It's a real tomb, with the body of a real soldier buried inside. The purpose of this monument is to honor the men who died fighting for America in the First World War. Congress decided in 1921 to build the monument in Arlington National Cemetery. So they sent a soldier to Europe to bring home the body of an American man who had died in the war and could not be identified. He would represent all the soldiers, known and unknown, who had given their lives for their country.

The Navy ship *Olympia* brought the body to Washington on November 9th, 1921. The U.S. Cavalry band played "Onward Christian Soldiers" as the casket was taken to the U.S. Capitol, where the soldier was laid in state.

"Taps" being played at the Tomb of the Unknown Soldier, November 11, 1921.

Office of History, U.S. Army Corps of Engineers: http://www.flickr.com/photos/usaceh q/6163007015/

President Warren G. Harding, governmental officials, and thousands of Americans paid their respects to this fallen soldier. On the morning of November 11th, this soldier was given a military procession to Arlington National Cemetery and buried at what is known today as the Tomb of the Unknown Soldier. The tomb has been guarded by American servicemen and women who honor the memory of our fallen soldiers so much that they have never left their post, even through two hurricanes that have happened in the years since the Unknown Soldier came home.

Text on the west face of the Tomb of the Unknown Soldier:
"Here rests in honored glory an American soldier known but to God"

Western panel; photo by Tim Evanson, http://www.flickr.com/photos/23165290@N00/7102836773/in/photostream/

Let's remember to honor veterans on Veterans' Day. If you know a veteran, remember to say thank-you.

Tomb of the Unknown Soldier: U.S. Army images: army.mil-56011-2009-11-13-091110

The Tomb of the Unknown Soldier, Arlington National Cemetery, Washington, D.C.

Fourth Thursday in November
Thanksgiving Day

Today I'm going to share with you a great old story, a true story. And it's a story that I have loved ever since I was a little boy about your age. It's the story of America's first Thanksgiving.

When I was a boy, every American boy and girl knew about the Pilgrims and the first Thanksgiving. But today, schools don't teach history as well as they used to, so some people believe things that aren't true about it. There are even some books that will tell you that the Pilgrims held the Thanksgiving feast at the end of their first harvest in Plymouth to give thanks to the Indians who had taught them to farm and fish in the New World. That's not true, of course. The feast was a celebration the Pilgrims held to give thanks to God for a bountiful harvest. They invited their friends the Indians to share their feast with them. For several days they gave thanks, feasted and played games together.

But to understand why the Pilgrims were so happy, we have to go back several years to England, the land the Pilgrims had come from. In England, King James I had been persecuting many Christians because they had their own churches and would not join the Church of England. The King was the head of the church in England and he wanted all Englishmen to be under his authority spiritually as well as being his citizens. Some Christians felt this was wrong according to the Bible and so they wouldn't join his church. They believed that churches should be independent of the government and choose their own pastors instead of having them picked by the King from his "approved" list.

King James I of England

King James I portrait: Victoria and Albert Museum, London, England

These people were called "Dissenters." King James did not like them at all. He sent soldiers to break up their church meetings. He charged some of them big fines and put some of them in jail. Some had their property stolen and some were even killed. All for believing the Bible!

This had been going on for some years when, in 1609 a group of them left England and went to Holland where there was religious freedom. This group built a Christian community in Holland and settled down to live among the Dutch people. They established their own church and made homes for their families.

Holland

Pilgrims praying about leaving Holland

But after a while, these new settlers began to think of leaving Holland. William Bradford, who would one day be a governor of the Pilgrim colony in Massachusetts, wrote that they left Holland for two reasons: one reason was because they felt that the ungodly young people of Holland were a bad influence on their children. The other reason was that they wanted to establish a new society that was built on the principles of the Bible. They wanted to build this new society in a new land and share the gospel with the people who already lived there.

Pilgrims departing from England to go to the new world.

Britannica Online for Kids. Web. 9 July 2013. <http://kids.britannica.com/comptons/art-151087>

The *Mayflower II*, a replica of the original ship that brought the Pilgrims to America.

So in 1620, these believers left their homes in Holland and sailed back to England. There they joined up with some other Christians who had stayed in England but were finally ready to leave the homes they knew and go to a new land where they could worship as they chose and live in more freedom. They also wanted to get to know the Indians who already lived in America and teach them about Jesus.

The believers from Holland had bought a ship called the *Speedwell* and on July 22, sailed from Leiden, Holland to Southampton, England. There the combined group got on board the *Speedwell* and another ship, the *Mayflower,* and set sail for America in November of 1620. They ran into trouble right away. The *Speedwell* started leaking! They returned to England for repairs but it turned out that the *Speedwell* just wasn't a strong enough ship to be safe for a long voyage clear across the ocean.

So the Pilgrims and some other passengers, called "Strangers" by the Pilgrims, all crowded into the little *Mayflower* and sailed for two months across the Atlantic to the New World. It was a very hard trip. Everybody was crammed together with little chance to keep clean and get healthy exercise. The weather was bad, with lots of powerful storms that blew them far off course.

Finally, in December of 1620 the lookout spied land on the horizon. The Pilgrims had reached America! But they weren't in Virginia, where they had intended to go. The storm winds had blown them far north, to what is now Massachusetts. So there was no Jamestown Colony with houses and food and the other things they needed. The poor Pilgrims landed on a cold, bleak shore where no food or shelter or friends awaited them.

The women and children spent most of the next two months still living on the *Mayflower* with the captain and crew while the men built huts and cabins for them to live in on shore. They ran low on food. The men were unfamiliar with hunting and fishing in the New World, so it was hard to get more food for their families. So even after they moved into the cabins on shore, life was still very hard.

That first winter was a very sad time. Their new homes were poorly built, cold and drafty. The people were hungry. Many got sick. It was so bad that about half of

The Pilgrims' first winter in America, 1620-1621

the settlers died before spring came. How awful!

But finally it came and the Pilgrims got out the seeds they had brought from England and began to plant their gardens and fields. They met some friendly Indians and learned from them how to hunt and fish. They traded trinkets and tools to the Indians for food and other things they needed. One of the Indians, a young man named Squanto, was a great help as he showed them how to grow crops, fertilizing them with small fish caught from nearby waters.

Spring and summer passed. The Pilgrims had nearly starved in the early months of their settlement but now they began to eat the fruits of their fields and the game and fish they took from the forests, streams and ocean. They got to know the Indians better and made a peace treaty with them that lasted for over half a century.

Pilgrims met friendly Indians and made a peace treaty with them.

In the autumn, when the harvest had been gathered in, the Pilgrims found themselves better off than they had been in the entire time they had been in the New World. It had been a long, hard year but they had made it with God's help. They decided to dedicate a special feast for giving thanks to God for a good harvest.

Squanto: http://www.encyclopedia.com/topic/Squanto.aspx

Squanto, who spoke English, helped the Pilgrims.

The Pilgrims invited their Indian friends to eat with them and celebrate the harvest. The Indians brought some deer they had hunted in the forest to add to the feast. The celebration went on for days with feasting, prayers, games, and contests. The Pilgrims knew they still had hard times ahead of them, but God had brought them through the dark days of the voyage and the sad, hard winter when so many of their friends and loved ones had died. The Pilgrims were especially fond of Squanto, who had done so much to help them survive in their new home. When he died, he was greatly mourned by the English colonists. Governor William Bradford wrote in his diary that Squanto: "became a special instrument sent of God for [our] good . . . He showed [us] how to plant [our] corn, where to take fish and to procure other commodities . . . and was also [our] pilot to bring [us] to unknown places for [our] profit, and never left [us] till he died." When Squanto lay dying of a fever, Bradford wrote that their Indian friend "desir[ed] the Governor to pray for him, that he might go to the Englishmen's God in heaven."

The Pilgrims' feast may have been the first Thanksgiving celebration in America, but it was not the last. Although the holiday wasn't set on the fourth Thursday of November until the twentieth century, there have been many special days set aside for the giving of thanks to God in America. It has been celebrated each year since the Civil War.

I hope you have a wonderful Thanksgiving Day at your house this year. We will have a big celebration at my home, with my children and grandchildren. That's a big group! And as we give thanks for the many blessings that God has so kindly given us, one very special blessing for me is knowing that I have little buddies like you all across America listening to my recordings. Thank you for listening to me. I hope you will continue to do so for a long, long time. And maybe I'll get to meet you in person some time! I do travel around the country a lot, you know.

I'm thankful for you.

"The First Thanksgiving" was painted circa 1912-1915 by Jean Leon Gerome Ferris (1863-1930).

December 25
Christmas Day

Trinity United Methodist Church; http://rr-t.com/bookmark/1063597

Well, I guess Christmas time is about every kid's favorite time of the year. I'm too old to be a kid, but I love it too. And so does everybody at my house.

Christmas is a wonderful time because it's all about Christ. You might say that the greatest miracle in history was when Jesus came from heaven to live on earth as a man. Imagine—God the Son left heaven and came down to live among us. He had to put up with hunger, tiredness, pain and sin all around Him. We can only imagine how awful that must have been for the Holy One—to live among unholy people.

But Jesus did all this because He loved us. And that's why Christmas is so special. It is a yearly reminder of how much we are loved.

A lot of people don't understand what Christmas is about. They think it's about a legend called Santa Claus and getting presents. A lot of traditions have grown up around Christmas, fun things people do to celebrate the big holiday. Some of those things remind us of Jesus and the real meaning of the day. Other things are just fun to do as a part of the celebration.

As Christians, let's learn to think of all the happy traditions as reminders of Jesus. When you look at the lovely colored lights, remember that Jesus is the light of the world. When you look at your Christmas tree, remember that Jesus died on a cross made out of a tree. When you enjoy giving gifts to the people you love, remember that Jesus was the first Christmas gift—given by God to the world. Let's allow all the beautiful things of Christmas remind us that He is our beautiful Savior.

Now, here's the true Christmas story. Enjoy reading it with your family, as the Boyers do, every Christmas Day:

Roman Emperor Caesar Augustus

And it came to pass in those days, that there went out a decree from Caesar Augustus, that all the world should be taxed.

(And this taxing was first made when Cyrenius was governor of Syria.)

And all went to be taxed, every one into his own city.

And Joseph also went up from Galilee, out of the city of Nazareth, into Judaea, unto the city of David, which is called Bethlehem; (because he was of the house and lineage of David:) to be taxed with Mary his espoused wife, being great with child.

http://www.morethings.com/god_and_country/jesus/christmas_photo_gallery07.htm

And so it was, that, while they were there, the days were accomplished that she should be delivered.

And she brought forth her firstborn son, and wrapped him in swaddling clothes, and laid him in a manger; because there was no room for them in the inn.

http://www.lostseed.com/extras/free-graphics/images/jesus-pictures/birth-of-jesus.php

http://www.layoutsparks.com/1/175069/A-Sign-The-Shepherds-31000.htm

And there were in the same country shepherds abiding in the field, keeping watch over their flock by night.

And, lo, the angel of the Lord came upon them, and the glory of the Lord shone round about them: and they were sore afraid.

And the angel said unto them, "Fear not: for, behold, I bring you good tidings of great joy, which shall be to all people. For unto you is born this day in the city of David a Saviour, which is Christ the Lord.

"And this shall be a sign unto you; Ye shall find the babe wrapped in swaddling clothes, lying in a manger."

And suddenly there was with the angel a multitude of the heavenly host praising God, and saying, "Glory to God in the highest, and on earth peace, good will toward men."

And it came to pass, as the angels were gone away from them into heaven, the shepherds said one to another, "Let us now go even unto Bethlehem, and see this thing which is come to pass, which the Lord hath made known unto us."

And they came with haste, and found Mary, and Joseph, and the babe lying in a manger. And when they had seen it, they made known abroad the saying which was told them concerning this child.

And all they that heard it wondered at those things which were told them by the shepherds.

But Mary kept all these things, and pondered them in her heart. And the shepherds returned, glorifying and praising God for all the things that they had heard and seen, as it was told unto them.

And when eight days were accomplished for the circumcising of the child, his name was called JESUS, which was so named of the angel before he was conceived in the womb. And when the days of her purification according to the law of Moses were accomplished, they brought him to Jerusalem, to present him to the Lord;

(As it is written in the law of the Lord, Every male that openeth the womb shall be called holy to the Lord;)

And to offer a sacrifice according to that which is said in the law of the Lord, a pair of turtledoves, or two young pigeons.

And, behold, there was a man in Jerusalem, whose name was Simeon; and the same man was just and devout, waiting for the consolation of Israel: and the Holy Ghost was upon him. And it was revealed unto him by the Holy Ghost, that he should not see death, before he had seen the Christ. And he came by the Spirit into the temple: and when the parents brought in the child Jesus, to do for him after the custom of the law, Then took he him up in his arms, and blessed God, and said,

"Lord, now lettest thou thy servant depart in peace, according to thy word: for mine eyes have seen thy salvation, which thou hast prepared before the face of all people; a light to lighten the Gentiles, and the glory of thy people Israel."

http://www.morethings.com/god_and_country/jesus/christmas_photo_gallery07.htm

And Joseph and his mother marvelled at those things which were spoken of him.

And Simeon blessed them, and said unto Mary his mother, "Behold, this child is set for the fall and rising again of many in Israel; and for a sign which shall be spoken against; (Yea, a sword shall pierce through thy own soul also,) that the thoughts of many hearts may be revealed."

And there was one Anna, a prophetess, the daughter of Phanuel, of the tribe of Aser: she was of a great age, and had lived with an husband seven years from her virginity; and she was a widow of about fourscore and four years, which departed not from the temple, but served God with fastings and prayers night and day. And she coming in that instant gave thanks likewise unto the Lord, and spake of him to all them that looked for redemption in Jerusalem.

And when they had performed all things according to the law of the Lord, they returned into Galilee, to their own city Nazareth. And the child grew, and waxed strong in spirit, filled with wisdom: and the grace of God was upon him.

Now when Jesus was born in Bethlehem of Judaea in the days of Herod the king, behold, there came wise men from the east to Jerusalem, saying, "Where is he that is born King of the Jews? for we have seen his star in the east, and are come to worship him."

When Herod the king had heard these things, he was troubled, and all Jerusalem with him.

And when he had gathered all the chief priests and scribes of the people together, he demanded of them where Christ should be born.

And they said unto him, "In Bethlehem of Judaea: for thus it is written by the prophet, 'And thou Bethlehem, in the land of Juda, art not the least among the princes of Juda: for out of thee shall come a

Wise Men speaking with King Herod

http://commons.wikimedia.org/wiki/File:Brooklyn_Museum_-_The_Magi_in_the_House_of_Herod_%28Les_rois_mages_chez_H%C3%A9rode%29_-_James_Tissot.jpg

Governor, that shall rule my people Israel.' "

Then Herod, when he had privily called the wise men, enquired of them diligently what time the star appeared.

And he sent them to Bethlehem, and said, "Go and search diligently for the young child; and when ye have found him, bring me word again, that I may come and worship him also."

When they had heard the king, they departed; and, lo, the star, which they saw in the east, went before them, till it came and stood over where the young child was.

When they saw the star, they rejoiced with exceeding great joy.

And when they were come into the house, they saw the young child with Mary his mother, and fell down, and worshipped him: and when they had opened their treasures, they presented unto him gifts; gold, and frankincense, and myrrh.

And being warned of God in a dream that they should not return to Herod, they departed into their own country another way.

painting by Eugene-Alexis Girardet Museum Syndicate: http://www.museumsyndicate.com/item.php?item=49138

And when they were departed, behold, the angel of the Lord appeareth to Joseph in a dream, saying, "Arise, and take the young child and his mother, and flee into Egypt, and be thou there until I bring thee word: for Herod will seek the young child to destroy him."

When he arose, he took the young child and his mother by night, and departed into Egypt:

And was there until the death of Herod: that it might be fulfilled which was spoken of the Lord by the prophet, saying, "Out of Egypt have I called my son."

Isn't that a wonderful story? And the best thing is, it's all true. The miracle of Christmas is a better, happier, more wonderful thing than any other Christmas story or movie you've ever heard of. It's a story that never grows old and will last as long as the love of God.

The reason Christmas is so wonderful is that Jesus' birth was just the beginning. Jesus came to earth as a baby. He grew into a man, but He was still God as well. He entered a world that was dirty and ugly because of our sin. But when the right time came, He died on a cross for your sins and mine. And now, if we repent of our sins and trust in Him, we can be in heaven with Him forever.

Merry Christmas, little buddies!

Uncle Rick's Christmas Story is from Luke 2:1-40, and Matthew 2:1-13, KJV

Ideas for Meaningful Celebrations

—Marilyn

I have been thinking of how to celebrate our holidays to show my family the true significance of the holiday. This book was born as part of that process. So many of our holidays are becoming secularized and we've forgotten the reason we began celebrating them as a nation in the first place. We pray that God will use this little book to help you as you seek to bring meaningful traditions into your home.

George Washington's Birthday

- We listen to Uncle Rick's *True Story of George Washington,* a wonderful story written in the 1800's. Consider making up a fun quiz seeing who can remember facts about Washington learned from listening to the story.
- Read Washington's Farewell Address, which references God and the Bible. It is our duty to teach the story of this leader who sought God in prayer for direction.
- Make a cake to celebrate the birthday of our first President.
- There are two stories about George Washington in *Profiles of Valor* (www.CharacterConcepts.com) that would be great to read together as a family.

Resurrection of Jesus

- The Empty Tomb: We do this every year at Easter to help the kids visualize the Empty Tomb.

Recipe:
4 c. flour
1 c. salt
1½ c. warm water

Mix flour and salt. Add water and mix until dough no longer sticks to the sides of the bowl. Then knead the dough on lightly floured surface until smooth. Roll out to about ½-inch thickness. Use a small oven proof bowl (glass is fine) turned upside down on cookie sheet. We spray the outside of the bowl with cooking spray so the tomb won't stick. Cover the bowl with the dough and make a finished edge at the bottom. Cut out a door "stone" to place up against the finished tomb. Place the stone face down on cookie sheet. Bake in warm oven (150°) for about 2 hours.When cool carefully remove the tomb from the bowl.

We place a piece of construction paper underneath the tomb with the words "He is not here, He has risen as He said." Place in a visible location for the Easter season.

- We always read a good Bible story book about the Resurrection.
- During the Easter season we read the Biblical account of the Passion week beginning with Jesus' Triumphal Entry into Jerusalem.

- Play music about the cross and the resurrection often, especially around Easter time. Joni Eareckson Tada's *Passion Hymns for a Kid's Heart* is a great resource.
- Here's a new twist on the Resurrection Cookie idea for Easter you can do with your kids/grandkids in order for them to understand the death and resurrection of Jesus Christ. This fun recipe uses crescent rolls and a disappearing marshmallow!

Preheat oven to 350°.
Ingredients:
Crescent rolls
Melted butter
Large marshmallows
Cinnamon
Sugar

Give each child a triangle of crescent rolls. The crescent roll represents the cloth that Jesus was wrapped in. *Read Matthew 27:57-61.*

1. Give each child a marshmallow. This represents Jesus.
2. Have him/her dip the marshmallow in melted butter. This represents the oils of embalming.
3. Now dip the buttered marshmallow in the cinnamon and sugar which represents the spices used to anoint the body.
4. Then wrap up the coated marshmallow tightly in the crescent roll (not like a typical crescent roll up, but bring the sides up and seal the marshmallow inside.) This represents the wrapping of Jesus' body after death.
5. Place in a 350° oven for 10-12 minutes. (The oven represents the tomb—pretend it's been three days!)
6. Let the rolls cool slightly. The children can open their rolls (cloth) and discover that Jesus is no longer there, HE IS RISEN! (The marshmallow melts and the crescent roll is puffed up, but empty.)

Now read Matthew 28:5-8.

Explain: At the tomb, Mary Magdalene and the other Mary saw an angel, who told them not to be afraid. No one had taken Jesus' body, but He had risen from the dead! The angel told the women to go and tell the disciples what they had seen, that Jesus had risen from the dead. They were so excited, they ran all the way home to tell the disciples the good news! He is risen from the dead! Alleluia!

Major Wooldridge at the Vietnam Memorial in Washington D.C. telling us about his men who lost their lives while preserving freedom.

MEMORIAL DAY

- Take a trip to the War Memorials in Washington D.C. It would be a fantastic way to spend Memorial Day. If you don't live near D.C. you could get a book to read about them.
- Take a trip to a Civil War or Revolutionary War battleground if you have one near you.
- Invite a veteran of any war to your house and ask him to tell you stories of his experiences defending our country and the stories of those with whom he served.
- Read a biography of someone who served and gave his life for our country during any of the wars in which our country has been involved.

FLAG DAY

- Do you fly a U.S. flag? If not, this would be a great day to begin doing so.
- Get a book about Betsy Ross and the design of our first flag.
- Get a book about flag etiquette.
- Have the children draw a picture of our first flag with 13 stars and stripes on it. We were given a flag with 13 stars on it by an elderly friend and treasure it greatly.

INDEPENDENCE DAY

Independence Day is one of my favorite holidays. John Adams said,

> The second day of July, 1776, will be the most memorable epoch in the history of America. I am apt to believe that it will be celebrated by succeeding generations as the great anniversary festival. It ought to be commemorated as the day of deliverance, by solemn acts of devotion to God Almighty. It ought to be solemnized with pomp and parade, with shows, games, sports, guns, bells, bonfires, and illuminations, from one end of this continent to the other, from this time forward forever more.

We now celebrate on July 4, but July 2 was known as Deliverance Day to the founders.

- We always have a big cookout (lots of great food) and invite lots of friends.
- We pass out statements about the sacrifices that some of the signers made for our freedom and have our guests and family members each read one to help us remember what these men willingly did on our behalf. Here are some you are welcome to use. You'll find more in *For You They Signed* by Marilyn Boyer.

Francis Lewis of NY—The British burned Lewis' home in September, 1776, seized his aging wife, and held her in a prison with no bed and no change of clothes. She was finally released two years later, but her health was gone and she died shortly thereafter.

Philip Livingston of NY—Livingston's 150,000 acre estate was seized by the British, but he continued to contribute his dwindling fortune to Congress for the war effort. The physical strain of the revolution took a toll on his health and he died less than two years after signing.

Lewis Morris of NY—Morris' Westchester estate was ransacked and nearly 1,000 acres were burned. His home was destroyed, his cattle butchered, and his family driven from their home.

John Hart of NJ—Father of 13 children, he was tending to his ailing wife he was told the British were coming to capture him. His neighbors promised to care for his wife and begged him to escape as he was too important to the cause. He fled to the woods where he lived for over a year. On returning to his home when the British retreated, he found it looted, burned, his wife had died and his children were scattered. He died shortly thereafter from the toll on his health.

Richard Stockton of NJ—Captured while rushing home to rescue his family, he was thrown into prison, where he was repeatedly beaten and nearly starved. The British destroyed his home and burned all his papers. As a result of his mistreatment, he became an invalid and died in 1781.

Arthur Middleton of SC—captured, and imprisoned after the British ravaged his plantation.

Thomas Heyward of SC—served in the army and was taken prisoner. The British raided his plantation and burned his buildings. His wife became ill and died before he was released.

Carter Braxton of VA—saw virtually every merchant ship he owned sunk or captured. He lost his wealth and was forced to sell his land.

William Ellery of RI—had his Newport home burned.

William Paca of MD—poured thousands of his own dollars into clothing American soldiers.

Robert Morris of PA—personally gave over two million dollars to the cause. He personally funded Washington's crossing the Delaware and Yorktown. He spent his later years in debtor's prison.

Thomas McKean of DE—reported that he was "hunted like a fox" during the revolution and at one time he was "compelled to move [his] family five times in a few months."

Caesar Rodney of DE—chose to stay in America and fight for freedom rather than go to England to seek a cure for his skin cancer. He was absent from Congress when the resolution for independence was being voted on. Returning home at night, he received a message from Thomas McKean: he was needed to cast the deciding vote for independence. He jumped on his horse without even taking time to change his clothes and rode 80 miles through a driving thunderstorm stopping only to change horses. As John Hancock rose to open the session, in came Rodney, all wet and bedraggled. He sank to his seat and rose to cast the vote that called for OUR independence!

Most of the signers of the Declaration of Independence made statements clarifying the fact that they were born-again Christians. We pass out some of these personal declarations of what they believed about Jesus Christ and have them read as well, to show the truth of our godly heritage in this country. Here is a sampling you can use. Lots more are contained in *For You They Signed.*

Samuel Adams: "I rely on the merits of Jesus Christ for a pardon for all my sins."

Charles Carroll: "On the mercy of my Redeemer I rely for salvation and on His merits; not on the works I have done in obedience to His precepts."

John Witherspoon: "I entreat you in the most earnest manner to believe in Jesus Christ, for there is salvation in no other."

Robert Treat Paine: "I am constrained to express my adoration of…the Author of my existence, in full belief of ... His forgiving mercy revealed to the world through Jesus Christ, through whom I hope for never ending happiness in a future state."

Benjamin Rush: "My only hope of salvation is in the infinite, transcendent love of God manifested to the world by the death of His son upon the Cross. Nothing but His blood will wash away my sins."

Roger Sherman: "I believe that there is only one living and true God, existing in three persons, the Father, the Son and the Holy Ghost.. and that at the end of the world, there will be a resurrection from the dead, and a final judgment of all mankind, when the righteous shall be publically acquitted before Christ the Judge, and be admitted to everlasting life and glory, and the wicked be sentenced to everlasting punishment."

- I ask one of our sons to read the speech given by Patrick Henry to the signers urging them to sign the document even if it was with last drop of their blood.
- One of our sons or guests will be chosen to read the Declaration of Independence.
- We honor those attending who are veterans or current members of the armed forces.
- Sometimes our younger children put on a parade singing about our country. This year my youngest daughter led the grandkids in acting out petitioning to King George and then the signing of the Declaration of Independence. We got costumes and they learned their lines which were actual words the signers spoke.
- We listen to Uncle Rick's Independence Day story. We often have a new Uncle Rick CD to pass out to children attending.
- Our son Nate dresses up like Uncle Sam and passes candy out to all the children, and books or CD's to each family.

Let us remember what Independence Day is all about and make an impression on our children and guests!

Star Spangled Banner Day

- Read the story of the writing of the Star Spangled Banner. Print out all the verses and sing as a family. It tells the whole story within the four verses.

- Invite some friends over for dinner and read and sing with them. Many people don't know the story and it's important that we share with others.
- Read a biography about Francis Scott Key and the Battle of Fort McHenry. We're excited to offer a fabulous book no longer in print as an e-book on our site. It is meant for reading level 2-4 grade, but younger and older children will definitely enjoy the story as well: *Francis Scott Key • Poet and Patriot.*

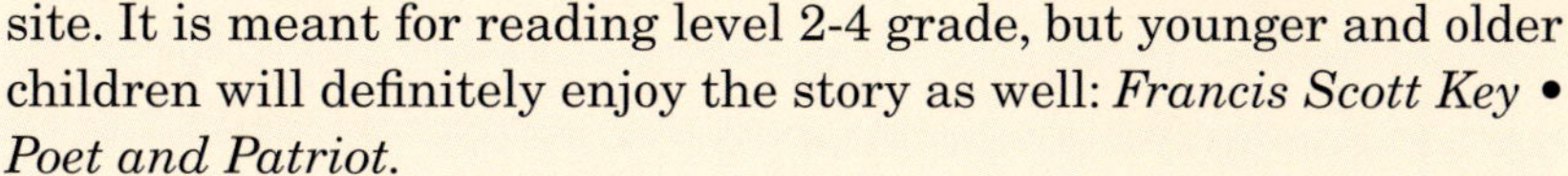

Columbus Day

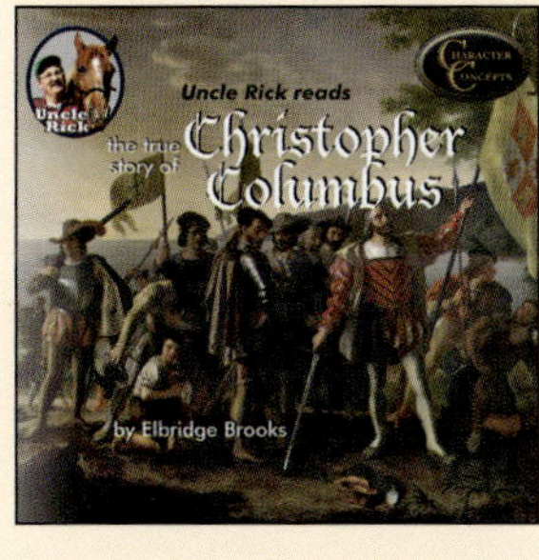

- Listen to Uncle Rick's *The True Story of Columbus,* an audio of a book written in the 1800's before revisionist history.
- Read a good book about Christopher Columbus. We recommend *Christopher Columbus—Adventurer of Faith and Courage* by Bennie Rhodes. It's part of the Sower Series.
- For young adults we recommend Dr. John Eidsmoe's book, *Columbus & Cortez, Conquerors for Christ.*

Veterans' Day

- Restaurants in many towns have "Vets eat free" night on Veteran's Day. We love to go out to eat that night (Rick is a vet himself) and then look for a vet sitting all by himself and strike up a conversation with him.
- I have a friend who will pay for the meal of any veteran she sees in a restaurant throughout the year. That is a fantastic way to show them honor.

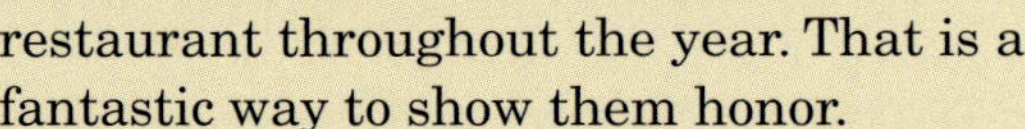

- Invite a veteran to your home for dinner. Ask him of his experience while in the service. Your kids will learn in a way they'll never forget and you can show him honor as well.

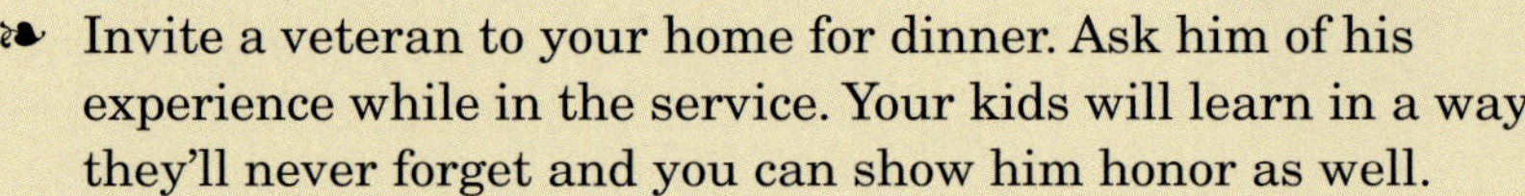

- Send a card of appreciation to a vet thanking him for his service to our country.

Thanksgiving Day

I used to be concerned that Thanksgiving would get lost with the prospect of Christmas coming, so we thought of ways to put Thanksgiving in its proper place first.

- Our younger children dress up in their pilgrim and Indian costumes to help us remember the heritage the Pilgrims left us.

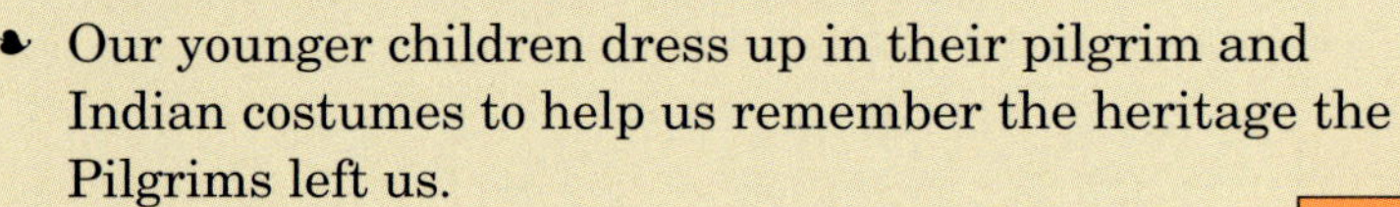

- We listen to Stories of the Pilgrims that Rick recorded for the kids, learning of Squanto's life and how he was used as an instrument in the hand of God on behalf of the Pilgrims.
- Make a wreath to show our gratefulness to God and then use that wreath as the main wreath of our Christmas celebrations that year. Everyone has their name on one of the gingerbread boys and on the back they wrote something they were thankful to God for that had occurred in the past year.

  Every year we creatively plan a new wreath. One year we used miniatures to represent notable occurrences in each one's life during the year, such as a new baby, a marriage, Tuck shooting his first deer, etc. One year we had colorful balls on which we wrote in glitter glue something we were thankful for.
- Begin a time capsule. It's a record of goals set and goals accomplished, and reflections on notable things that happened since the last Thanksgiving. You can change the form every year. We store everyone's form in a old popcorn container in the attic until next year. Each person reads his own to see if they met their goals and be reminded of how God has blessed their life. Older siblings or parents can help the little ones fill out one, too. It's great to see how your young ones will answer questions like "What is a lesson God has taught you this year?"
- Make a special tablecloth to use on Thanksgiving Day. We have all the family and any guests sign it and write something they are thankful for. (We often invite people to spend Thanksgiving with us who have no family in town).

- Read a book about the true story of the first Thanksgiving. *Thanksgiving, A Time to Remember* is great for use throughout the month of November. It includes an abbreviated narrative for very young children. We have found, though, on the actual Thanksgiving day we need to keep it simple as we have 33 family members present at our celebration, 11 of those being 8 years and under! So, this year, Rick has written an "Uncle Rick Tells the Story of the First Thanksgiving" (the story in this book) to read during our family celebration. Hope you enjoy it.

- Make place cards (decorated with stickers) for each person present at our table. Instead of the person's name, we write a Scripture verse that deals with thankfulness, highlighting things for which the Scriptures tell us to acknowledge our thankfulness to God and others. At the completion of our meal, we'll go around the table in order, having each person read the verse in front of them. We then ask some simple questions to help everyone focus on the meaning and application of the Scriptures.

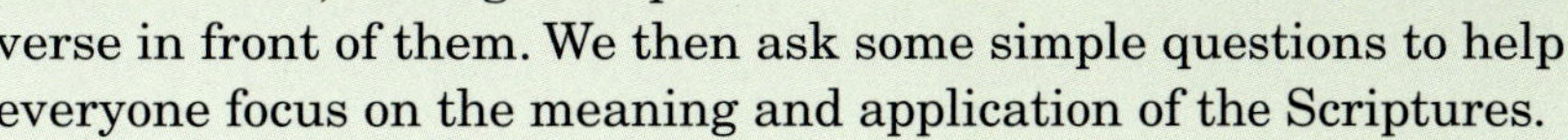

Christmas

Christmas is about the Gospel. Christmas is also a time of year that is full of opportunities to share this good news. I have listed just a few ideas that you might find doable for your family this season. These are activities and projects that have become traditions in our family each Christmas. Maybe at least one of these will spark your interest. Include your whole family. Take the time to do it!

- Every year we make Christmas cookies and take them to the Emergency Services people in our community, volunteer fire departments, sheriff's departments, rescue squad. We include a note to express our appreciation and to thank them for their services in behalf of our community as well as a gospel tract.
- Each year we make nativity cookies for neighbors, a Christmas card and gospel tract. We had one lady to whose Dad we have given these cookies for years, and who is not a Christian, tell us how he always tells her we've come and how that opens the door to her to share the gospel again with him. The past couple of years we make cookies and take them to veterans as well. We've focused on World War II vets as they won't be with us many more years. It's a great way to honor them and open a door to share the gospel.
- It has been our tradition to try to find a family who is struggling financially at Christmas time, maybe a single mom or a family whose dad's been out of work, or a family who has a child with leukemia or another life-threatening

disease and bring presents for each family member. Each person chooses a gift for one of them. Young children can make them gifts as well. Again, it's a fabulous way to share the gospel.

- We have in years past gone Christmas caroling to shut-ins in their home or even the nursing home. It means so much to them! We usually combine the singing with bringing them a Christmas treat—cookies, a poinsetta, etc.
- During the years when we had lots of neighbors with young children, our children would deliver a wrapped *Picture Bible* to each household that had young children. *The Picture Bible* is a great tool for sharing God's Word with another family in a non-threatening way. It was always received with gratitude and God only knows how it may have softened a child's heart to the gospel.

http://carsonandcarson.files.wordpress.com/2009/12/bonfire2jpg6.jpg

- Have a "Bonfire Christmas Party." For many years now we have enjoyed opening our home during the Christmas season. We invite lots of friends for supper and Christmas foods. Then we head out to the backyard bonfire where we sit on bales of hay and sing Christmas carols together. We usually have someone, often one of our pastor friends, share some thoughts about Christmas and how it should impact our lives. We love singing and often stay late into the night doing so around the bonfire. Christmas is a time to reflect on the sacrifice of Jesus on our behalf coming to the earth as newborn helpless babe. I guess we started this tradition as it was a great time for quiet reflection and then celebrating with our close friends.
- Have a Christmas Open House. As the years went by, we had so many people it was hard having them all at one time, so we also began having a Christmas Open House, later in the season. We open our home one evening and friends can come and go when convenient. The girls love entertaining, baking, and decorating and it's such a great way to show hospitality to many folks at one time and give our family the privilege of serving them as our guests.

http://www.wallsave.com/wallpaper/1024x768/sleigh-ride-free-screensavers-